Acting Edition

Evanston Salt Costs Climbing

by Will Arbery

∥SAMUEL FRENCH∥

Copyright © 2023 by Will Arbery
All Rights Reserved

"Angel From Montgomery"
Written by John Prine
WC Music Corp. (ASCAP) Obo Walden Music Inc.
and Sour Grapes Music Inc.
All Rights Reserved. Used By Permission.

EVANSTON SALT COSTS CLIMBING is fully protected under the copyright laws of the United States of America, the British Commonwealth, including Canada, and all member countries of the Berne Convention for the Protection of Literary and Artistic Works, the Universal Copyright Convention, and/or the World Trade Organization conforming to the Agreement on Trade Related Aspects of Intellectual Property Rights. All rights, including professional and amateur stage productions, recitation, lecturing, public reading, motion picture, radio broadcasting, television, online/digital production, and the rights of translation into foreign languages are strictly reserved.

ISBN 978-0-573-71066-7

www.concordtheatricals.com
www.concordtheatricals.co.uk

FOR PRODUCTION INQUIRIES

UNITED STATES AND CANADA
info@concordtheatricals.com
1-866-979-0447

UNITED KINGDOM AND EUROPE
licensing@concordtheatricals.co.uk
020-7054-7298

Each title is subject to availability from Concord Theatricals Corp., depending upon country of performance. Please be aware that *EVANSTON SALT COSTS CLIMBING* may not be licensed by Concord Theatricals Corp. in your territory. Professional and amateur producers should contact the nearest Concord Theatricals Corp. office or licensing partner to verify availability.

CAUTION: Professional and amateur producers are hereby warned that *EVANSTON SALT COSTS CLIMBING* is subject to a licensing fee. The purchase, renting, lending or use of this book does not constitute a license to perform this title(s), which license must be obtained from Concord Theatricals Corp. prior to any performance. Performance of this title(s) without a license is a violation of federal law and may subject the producer and/or presenter of such performances to civil penalties. Both amateurs and professionals considering a production are strongly advised to apply to the appropriate agent before starting rehearsals, advertising, or booking a theatre. A licensing fee must be paid whether the title(s) is presented for charity or gain and whether or not admission is charged. Professional/Stock licensing fees are quoted upon application to Concord Theatricals Corp.

This work is published by Samuel French, an imprint of Concord Theatricals Corp.

No one shall make any changes in this title(s) for the purpose of production. No part of this book may be reproduced, stored in a retrieval system, scanned, uploaded, or transmitted in any form, by any means, now known or yet to be invented, including mechanical, electronic, digital, photocopying, recording, videotaping, or otherwise, without the prior written permission of the publisher. No one shall share this title(s), or any part of this title(s), through any social media or file hosting websites.

For all inquiries regarding motion picture, television, online/digital and other media rights, please contact Concord Theatricals Corp.

MUSIC AND THIRD-PARTY MATERIALS USE NOTE

Licensees are solely responsible for obtaining formal written permission from copyright owners to use copyrighted music and/or other copyrighted third-party materials (e.g. artworks, logos) in the performance of this play and are strongly cautioned to do so. If no such permission is obtained by the licensee, then the licensee must use only original music and materials that the licensee owns and controls. Licensees are solely responsible and liable for clearances of all third-party copyrighted materials, including without limitation music, and shall indemnify the copyright owners of the play(s) and their licensing agent, Concord Theatricals Corp., against any costs, expenses, losses and liabilities arising from the use of such copyrighted third-party materials by licensees. For music, please contact the appropriate music licensing authority in your territory for the rights to any incidental music.

IMPORTANT BILLING AND CREDIT REQUIREMENTS

If you have obtained performance rights to this title, please refer to your licensing agreement for important billing and credit requirements.

EVANSTON SALT COSTS CLIMBING had its world premiere at the White Heron Theater in Nantucket, Massachusetts, on August 30, 2018. It was produced by New Neighborhood and Jay Alix & Una Jackman. It was directed by Dustin Wills. The scenic design was by Jean Kim, the lighting design was by Masha Tsimring, the sound design was by Tyler Kieffer, the costume design was by Seth Bodie, and the projection design was by Nicholas Hussong. The production stage manager was Hannah Wichmann. The cast was as follows:

BASIL . . . . Justin Kirk
PETER . . . . Howard Overshown
MAIWORM . . . . Keira Naughton
JANE JR. . . . . Rachel Sachnoff

EVANSTON SALT COSTS CLIMBING had its New York premiere at The New Group on November 14, 2022. It played in the Alice Griffin Jewel Box Theatre at the Pershing Square Signature Center. It was directed by Danya Taymor. The scenic design was by Matt Saunders, the lighting design was by Isabella Byrd, the sound design was by Mikaal Sulaiman, additional sound design was by Evan Cook, and the costume design was by Sarafina Bush. Choreography was by Tilly Evans-Krueger, and the voice and text coach was Gigi Buffington. The production stage manager was Rachel Denise April. The cast was as follows:

BASIL . . . . Ken Leung
PETER . . . . Jeb Kreager
MAIWORM . . . . Quincy Tyler Bernstine
JANE JR. . . . . Rachel Sachnoff

ACKNOWLEDGMENTS

Thank you to Danya. Wow, we did it. How? Love you. Thank you to the thing underneath everything. Thank you Rachel Sachnoff, Quincy Tyler Bernstine, Jeb Kreager, and Ken Leung, for going down into that feeling for us, over and over again. Thank you to Scott Elliott, Ian Morgan, Teresa Gozzo, Cam Camden, Victoria Keesee, and everyone at The New Group. Thank you to the Griffin at the Signature. Thank you Isabella Byrd, Sarafina Bush, Mikaal Sulaiman, Evan Cook, Joshua Yocom, Ann James, Gigi Buffington, Tilly Evans-Krueger, and Matt Saunders. Thank you Rachel April, Stephen Varnado, Sydneii Colter. Thank you Joan Sergay. Thank you Jacob Robinson. Thank you Justin Kirk, Keira Naughton, and Howard Overshown. Thank you Dustin Wills. Thank you Tyler Kieffer, Masha Tsimring, Jean Kim, Nicholas Hussong, Hannah Wichmann, and Seth Bodie. Thank you Thomas Bradshaw, John MacGregor, Olivier Sultan, Eva Dickerman, Elise Kibler, Jesse Armstrong, Kate Dakota Kremer, Rolin Jones, Adam O'Byrne, Una Jackman, Jay Alix, Rebecca Kitt, The White Heron, Robert Egan, Emily James, Shannon Cochran, Casey Stangl, Jess Chayes, Ben Beckley, Michael Shannon, Larry Powell, and Ned Eisenberg. Thank you, John Prine! And thank you, Yi Huang. You got me through. You seeing this play, seeing what it was, got me through. I love you. So many more people. (All there ever was was people.) But one particular person more than any. Rachel, thanks for being my best friend. This book is dedicated to you, aslt.

CHARACTERS

BASIL – male, Greek, salt truck driver, 50s
PETER – male, Evanstonian, salt truck driver, 40s
MAIWORM – female, Evanstonian, public works administrator, 50s
JANE JR. – female, Evanstonian, volunteer, 20s

SETTING

Evanston, IL

TIME

Three Januarys
2014
2015
2016

AUTHOR'S NOTE

The **LADY IN THE PURPLE HAT** appears three times.
She wears a wide-brimmed felt purple hat and an old-flowers dress.
The first time, she's played by the actor playing Jane Jr.
The second time, she's played by the actor playing Maiworm.
The third time, she's played by the actor playing Peter.

2014

(The break room at the Evanston salt dome. **PETER** *and* **BASIL** *are drinking coffee.* **BASIL** *is reading from a sheet of paper.)*

BASIL. "That summer seemed to last forever. The whole family had been cursed since. Now it wasn't so much a legend as real life. The girl stopped running. As she stopped to catch her breath, she looked back. As she searched, her movements were frantic." The end.

PETER. I like it.

BASIL. Thanks.

PETER. Wait, that's how it ends?

BASIL. Yeh.

PETER. I like it.

BASIL. Thanks.

PETER. I like how it takes place in summer.

BASIL. Yeh.

PETER. Wha'd you do last night?

BASIL. I made a big salad but it was gross. Then for a while, you know, for a pretty long time, I stood at my kitchen window and played with my dick.

PETER. Yeah. I feel that. Did I tell you about the hot tub?

BASIL. No.

PETER. The hot tub's too small for anyone to use. I'm gonna get rid of the hot tub. Hot tubs have zero value.

PETER. It's like selling used toothbrushes. Basil, I want to kill myself.

(*Pause.*)

BASIL. You want to end your life?

PETER. Yeah.

BASIL. Well, don't.

(**MAIWORM** *enters.*)

MAIWORM. Listen to this. They wrote an article about us!

(*She holds up the newspaper and reads.*)

"EVANSTON SALT COSTS CLIMBING. By Bill Agrigento. Relentless winter storms are driving Evanston's salt costs to approximately $500,000, officials reported in a memo. Evanston city staff will ask aldermen on Monday to approve a purchase of rock salt in the amount of $70,128 from Morton Salt. Evanston Public Works Director Jackie Thorstensen and Assistant Director *Jane Maiworm* wrote in the memo –"

PETER. Oh...!

BASIL. Ho ho...!

PETER. Mentioned by name.

BASIL. Maiworm here in the paper.

PETER. Maiworm over here. Congratulations Maiworm.

MAIWORM. Thanks ah well it's nothing. But what am I gonna say, that it's not nice? It's nice. Usually in these I'm just *an official,* and meanwhile it's *Jackie Thorstensen said,* and *Jackie Thorstensen said.*

BASIL. Right!

MAIWORM. Anyway.

BASIL. Right!

MAIWORM. Anyway. "'Unfortunately due to an early snowfall in November and an active December,' Thorstensen and Maiworm reported –"

BASIL & PETER. Maiworm over here!

MAIWORM. "'Unfortunately due to an early snowfall in November and an active December,' Thorstensen and Maiworm reported, staff needed to spend an additional $70,128 'to ensure salt supplies were not depleted going into the heaviest snow fall of the season thus far, on Dec. 31.'"

BASIL. Right. Hoo-hoo!

MAIWORM. "Officials had reported earlier that snow removal costs are climbing. The city spent a total of $411,261 through the first two big storms of the year, on Dec. 31, and last week's blizzard on Jan. 4. $232,418 of that was for overtime (THAT'S YOU!). Miscellaneous costs included overtime (THAT'S YOU!) for tree removals and pothole repairs, which were needed as a result of the frigid temperatures, officials said." Pretty cool, huh fellows?

BASIL. Interesting, for sure. I didn't know the costs were climbing.

PETER. I knew the costs were climbing. I mean it makes sense.

BASIL. I mean it makes sense, but I didn't know they could climb so high. What does that do to everything?

MAIWORM. Well, it's a pressure on everyone. It's a sharper pressure.

BASIL. More work for us.

MAIWORM. More work for us, exactly.

PETER. But that article isn't really about us, no offense. "Overtime" is not my name. They should write a thing about what's it like on the roads, with the salt.

BASIL. What do you mean what it's like?

PETER. Like about what it's like out there when we're salting the roads.

BASIL. No one wants to read that. We drive, we salt. The end. Stories gotta have...like, pull.

MAIWORM. I agree.

PETER. Pool?

BASIL. Pull to pull you in.

MAIWORM. Pull you in exactly. This article's a little more administrative which I think is cool.

PETER. I think it's cool when we salt the roads. Sometimes people honk at us. Things fall down. The light's always changing. I think the noises when it hits the road is good. We have funny conversation in the front. It's cold. It's –

MAIWORM. Hahahaha yep. Well. Fun day already! Uh-oh. You guys gotta hit the road in like four minutes.

BASIL & PETER. Alright Maiworm.

(**MAIWORM** *exits.*)

PETER. We get an article written about us and that's what they write. They don't even have our names in it. Fucking Maiworm gets her name in it. I was just trying to think about how it might be cool to have a thing about Peter and Basil. A story, but instead of written with words, it's written with sounds and ice, that tell the story of Peter and Basil.

BASIL. Get over it. America is upsessed with names. In Greece no one gets names written about. We just live and have meals and do normal human drama. Without worrying about is like: is it fantastic human drama?

PETER. Isn't Greece where all the Drama started?

BASIL. Yeh but now we're so over it.

PETER. Well I'm sorry this isn't Greece.

BASIL. Me too, so. Because. It's warm there.

PETER. Well I'm sorry Evanston is cold.

BASIL. Me too.

(They drink coffee.)

PETER. My daughter's writing a story about me.

BASIL. Oh yeh? What about?

PETER. Just, fuckin…about me.

BASIL. Huh. I don't think your daughter's story would have much by way of…like, what, pull.

PETER. Fuck you

BASIL. No fuck you haha

PETER. Fuck you

BASIL. No fuck you

PETER. Fuck you haha

BASIL. No fuck you

PETER. Fuck you

BASIL. No fuck you

PETER. Fuck you haha

BASIL. No fuck you

PETER. Fuck you

BASIL. Okay hahaha.

PETER. I'm gonna kill you motherfucker I'm gonna fuck you up.

BASIL. No you won't I'm too pretty.

PETER. Pretty how.

BASIL. Just pretty.

PETER. Pretty in what way.

BASIL. Just a pretty guy.

PETER. Hahahaha.

BASIL. Hahaha.

PETER. FUCK laughing. I can't even look my wife in the eyes. The sight of my daughter depresses me. I know she's not gonna be very smart and it just seems like she's gonna become one of those chubby women who work at like a library or a church. That's just how it seems to me. Like a 99% prophecy. And it makes me wanna kill myself.

BASIL. Come on. Stop. Rude.

PETER. Rude to who?

BASIL. To those women.

PETER. It's not rude. Fuck you. Those women are fine. She can be one of them. It's fine. It just makes me wanna kill myself.

BASIL. Yeh. Okay. Peter.

PETER. Nevermind. Fuck me. Sorry.

BASIL. Okay no. Mmmmmmmm okay listen. Okay. Let me just try to. Okay. You're reminding me so much of. Nevermind. Mmm. Hm. Yeh. No I mean. Right right right.

PETER. Yeah?

BASIL. I mean, it's...it's it's it's. Yeh it's definitely hard. Even in Greece. On good days. Pretty days in the sun. Nobody leaves you alone. So you'd just look around and sometimes wanna kinda die. I know. But. At the end of the, whole. It's just. "Come on." Yeh?

PETER. No I mean that makes sense.

BASIL. Yeh, just a little...you know, you know who you are. And today's. But today will be better. Hahaha, but. You know we'll have good times in the truck.

PETER. True true true true true.

BASIL. Are you still feeling sadness?

PETER. A little. I can't help it. Are you?

BASIL. No.

PETER. Thanks for trying to cheer me up but it takes a while to sink in. My toes are cold.

BASIL. It's a cold day.

PETER. Negative seventeen. Butta time. Suppa time for us. Butta time.

BASIL. Butta time

PETER. Okay but have you thought about what it would be like to die?

BASIL. Like what, or like what, the feeling?

PETER. The feeling, yeah, of the dying, when it happens, what's going on in your heart or brain.

BASIL. Peter, are you asking me to go down into that feeling with you?

(**MAIWORM** *enters.*)

MAIWORM. Oh no. I have some bad news and it's bad.

PETER. Okay.

MAIWORM. Bill Agrigento killed himself this morning.

BASIL. Oh no.

PETER. Who the fuck is Bill Agrigento?

MAIWORM. He's the guy who wrote the article about us.

BASIL. Oh no.

PETER. "Evanston Salt Costs Climbing"?

MAIWORM. Yeah.

BASIL. Shit. Sad. Ah!

MAIWORM. We were the last thing he ever wrote about.

(*They let this sink in.*)

PETER. Is that why he did it?

MAIWORM. I have no possible idea, I don't know. Oh my God. I knew him. He was nice. He loved tea. He lived on Lee Street. He had a whole wall of different tea. He showed me a picture.

(**MAIWORM** *exits.*)

PETER. Goddamnit.

BASIL. What?

PETER. I wanted to kill myself and then Bill Agrigento did. There's nothing new that can be done.

BASIL. You thought killing yourself was a new thing that could be done?

PETER. I dunno, yeah.

BASIL. That is one of the oldest things to be done, I think, as a human activity.

PETER. Well so there's nothing new that can be done.

BASIL. There are new things that can be done.

PETER. Like what.

BASIL. I dunno. No one has ever done for example uh. This:

>*(**BASIL** goes up to **PETER**. He grabs **PETER**'s butt cheeks. He kneels down and talks into **PETER**'s butt.)*

Winter bunkfuck, all gas zebra, float off bumbleboy. Float away bumbleboy to a warmer sheeeeeeeen! Happen forever happen ever grip!

>*(**PETER** laughs and moves away. He gets really sad.)*

PETER. Fuck.

BASIL. What?

PETER. It just...it won't go away.

BASIL. Yeh. Fuck. Uh well. Yeh.

>*(**MAIWORM** enters.)*

MAIWORM. I just, hey guys. I just. I've been feeling really rattled by this news, and I just wanted to say: I appreciate everything that you are in my life. You always have a home, in me. And if you ever need anything, please talk to me. You're good men. And.

BASIL & PETER. Thanks Maiworm.

>*(**MAIWORM** nods a lot. Then she takes a deep breath. We hear the sound of a salt truck backing into the warehouse. She looks at her watch.)*

MAIWORM. Oh, you should probably hit the road. And I should head over to the office. This *day*. This –

>*(She leaves.)*

PETER. We should get on the road.

BASIL. Yeh.

(They get ready to leave.)

Peter, it's pretty simple, you need to be a little more okay with –

PETER. Shut the fuck up, honestly, Basil. You've been patronizing as fuck to me all morning. Ah. Sorry.

BASIL. That's uh

PETER. Uh. I love your story, though. About summer. Really. You should do something with that.

*(They head out. **BASIL** leaves first. As he exits, **PETER** slaps his own face, hard, over and over.)*

(Now:)

*(**MAIWORM** is standing outside in her nightgown and slippers. **JANE JR.** comes outside wrapped in a blanket. There is a snowstorm happening.)*

JANE JR. Mom? What are you doing out here? It's freezing!

MAIWORM. Oh I'm sorry Jane Jr., I was having the most horrible dream. Go back to bed.

JANE JR. What happened in the dream?

MAIWORM. It was – oh gosh, sorry but, to be honest it was about the dead. All the dead. They were rising up in a blurry chorus, and Bill Agrigento was getting fused into them. It was scary.

JANE JR. The guy who killed himself? Well now I'm gonna have nightmares about that!

MAIWORM. But then it became about heated permeable pavers.

JANE JR. What are that? Is those.

MAIWORM. Well they're... nevermind, they're a new technology. I can't get them out of my head.

JANE JR. *(Shuddering from the cold.)* What're they for?

MAIWORM. Well don't worry. They're roads that heat themselves. They're de-icing technology. Permeable paving is paving that lets the water, when it rains, fall on top of it and drain right through to the ground, through to the ground below. The surface is both smooth *and* porous. They invented it so that rainwater didn't have to go through the gutter and all the way under the city and all the way off-site for treatment. But *heated* permeable pavers are permeable pavers with heat things under them. So you can imagine what this means.

JANE JR. I can?

MAIWORM. It means that during ice storms, the ice melts right away, and the water goes right down into the ground, instead of remaining on the surface and refreezing into ice. So it solves like fifty million problems at once. No more plowing except in extreme cases. No more salt. Anyway I've been looking into it, it's a task I gave myself. So you add all this up, and you can imagine what this means.

JANE JR. I don't know if I can.

MAIWORM. It's objectively better. Sorry to say. They're trying them out over in Rock Island and Davenport. They worked in Nebraska. And we've got some real curious parties. Polly from Northwestern is even interested in testing them out on campus. But gosh, Jane Jr., it would be such a big change. It'd put all the truck guys like Peter and Basil out of work. And imagine the construction. And do I trust a road like that? A ground like that? With little secret characters underneath it? Like is this Evanston or is this

Disneyton? Heated permeable pavers. I feel as though they're coming. And one day, acting upon the orders of the dead, they'll rise up from the ground and wrap around us until we – anyway. Just a dream. Just a little nervousness. How was your day?

JANE JR. It was okay. I helped out a lot at the nursing home.

MAIWORM. That's great. Did you sing?

JANE JR. Yeah I sang.

MAIWORM. What'd you sing?

JANE JR. "Angel from Montgomery." Dave Matthews Band version.

MAIWORM. Wish I could have heard it.

JANE JR. It wasn't very good.

MAIWORM. Oh, look, there go Peter and Basil in the salt truck. It must be late or early, wow! Wave!

(*They wave to them. A honk in response.*)

JANE JR. We should go inside. It's so cold.

MAIWORM. Yeah. They're calling it a polar vortex.

JANE JR. A bipolar vortex?

MAIWORM. No, a polar vortex. I hope everyone's safe on the roads tonight. I just worry for this town.

JANE JR. Okay but don't worry about the heated permeable pavers, Mom. They're not here yet. It's still salt right now for the roads.

MAIWORM. Anyhow.

(*She takes a deep breath. The wind roars.*)

It's still salt right now for the roads.

(*Now:*)

(**PETER** *and* **BASIL** *are in the salt truck. They're really cold.* **PETER** *is driving.*)

BASIL. I was thinking about writing another new story.

PETER. (*Coughing a little.*) Huh okm. Cool. Okahm. Sorry. Cool.

BASIL. Based on me, on real things of my life.

PETER. Oh yeah. Good good. Right.

(**PETER** *keeps checking the heat.*)

Does it feel like anything's coming out?

BASIL. It's coming, it's warming.

PETER. Hm. Hm. Fuck.

BASIL. It's warming, it's coming. Look.

PETER. Fuck. Yeah. Fuck.

BASIL. It is.

PETER. Hm.

BASIL. See.

PETER. Fuck.

BASIL. Feel it.

PETER. Fuck. Hm. I don't know. Fuck.

BASIL. See.

PETER. Okam

BASIL. Feel it.

PETER. Okam.

BASIL. Feel it. It's okay.

PETER. Yeah? No. Fuck.

(**BASIL** *realizes there's no heat coming out.*)

BASIL. Fuck.

PETER. Yeah.

BASIL. Fuck. Ah, fuck.

PETER. Yeah, see?

BASIL. Fuck. Fuck.

PETER. Yeah, fuck.

BASIL. I just fuck.

PETER. Yeah I don't think it is.

BASIL. Fuck. But it will.

PETER. I don't think it is.

BASIL. It will, it will, it always does.

PETER. I don't think it will. I don't think IT IS, BASIL.

BASIL. It will. Shh, it's fine, it is.

PETER. I don't know if IT IS, BASIL.

BASIL. Fuck.

PETER. Right?

BASIL. Fuck.

PETER. Right. Right.

BASIL. It might not.

PETER. Right.

BASIL. Fuck.

PETER. It broke. It fucking broke.

BASIL. But why would it break

PETER. The core could be

BASIL. What, clogged

PETER. The tubes could be

BASIL. Leaking?, what

PETER. There's no smell, there's a smell if it's leaking

BASIL. The fan maybe broke

PETER. Or the water froze

BASIL. But there's antifreeze

PETER. Or the antifreeze froze

BASIL. It shouldn't break, it cannot break

PETER. It broke

BASIL. No way, fuck no. The cold has entered my heart.

PETER. The cold has entered my heart. It's minus thirty.

BASIL. Thirty below. Hahaha.

PETER. "Feels like."

BASIL. "Feels like."

PETER. Feels like thirty fucking below.

BASIL. Hahaha "feels like," fuck

PETER. Hahahaha.

BASIL. *(Hyper-articulated.)* Hahahahaha, ha ha! Ha! Oh fuck, and an uh and an uh and a haha.

PETER. *(Hyper-articulated.)* Yes fuckin ha and a Ha and a Ha and a Bunkfuck.

BASIL. Hahahaha

PETER. Hahahaha FUCK laughing.

BASIL. FUCK laughing.

PETER. Hahahaha.

BASIL. Good.

PETER. Real good.

BASIL. Great stuff.

PETER. Real great stuff. Excellent stuff. Good material.

> *(He brakes suddenly. The sounds of skidding. They both gasp and brace. It's terrifying. Something thuds in the back. They steady.)*

Sorry.

BASIL. Ice. Ice is ice.

PETER. Ice is ice.

BASIL. Yeh. Yeh.

PETER. Yeah. Yeah. We gotta check the chute.

BASIL. Yeh?

PETER. Yeah, we gotta check the chute.

BASIL. Yeh?

PETER. *(Opening the door.)* Yeah I think we should – fuck, fuck – ah, fuck, the handle, feel fuck!

BASIL. Fuck.

PETER. Yeah fuck but we gotta check the

BASIL. Chute. Okay. Okay. Fuck. My balls, do you feel that?

PETER. Yeah my balls too.

BASIL. Me balls. Me chattering balls.

PETER. Me and my chattering balls, my chattering balls and me.

BASIL. Haha.

PETER. I ruined it. Dumb.

BASIL. Funny dumb!

PETER. You're too kind sir

BASIL. Sir you're too kind to a mere

PETER. To a mere truck man

BASIL. To a mere

PETER. Sir you're far too kind to a mere

BASIL. Sir you're far too kind

PETER. Ahhh okay let's

BASIL. Yeh let's

PETER. Ooooo okay

BASIL. Okay okay yeh ooooo okay AHHHHH

PETER. AHHHH FUCK AHHH OKAY OKAY OKAY

BASIL. OKAY OKAY

PETER & BASIL. *(Hyper-unison.)* AH OKAY OKAY FUCK FUCK OKAY FUCK HAHA AH FUCK OH OKAY AH

> *(They burst out of their doors. They fix the chute. They run back – freezing.* **PETER** *starts up the truck.)*

PETER. *(Shivering.)* See that garbage truck?

BASIL. *(Shivering.)* What garbage truck?

PETER. Not that truck, that other truck, the one behind us? That truck's been there a year and a half.

BASIL. It's hard to clean those trucks.

PETER. It is, it is hard to clean those trucks. Say things. Say things. Say your story.

BASIL. Say my story

Ah

Kay

Kay

Ah

BASIL. Kay

Kay

Ah

Kay

Hoo hoo hoo

My story is

This thing about how

Hoo hoo

OH wait

is it finally

is it

PETER. I think

(The heat's coming back on.)

BASIL. I think it's coming on –!

PETER. I think yeah!

BASIL. It is yeh –!

PETER. Yeah

BASIL. Yeh it is!

PETER. It is.

BASIL. Yes. Yeehaw. A yeehaw. And a yes.

PETER. Don't shh don't over-celebrate.

BASIL. Right.

PETER. Don't want to over-celebrate. It hates that.

BASIL. Right. Good. Thanks, truck, for the, thank you.

PETER. Right. Simple thanks. A simple thank you.

BASIL. A simple thank you. Thank you.

PETER. Thank you.

BASIL. Kay

Kay

So

My story is still in the storm phase.

Is that okay?

PETER. Sure.

BASIL. Kay. My story's about my yiayia, and about the lady in the purple hat. Believe it or not, I never touched my yiayia.

PETER. What's your yiayia?

BASIL. Yiayia is grandmother.

PETER. Oh okay, I thought it was your dick.

BASIL. No. So I do not touch my yiayia, ever. We never hugged. My yiayia was always sitting far away in rooms. Since the day my parents found me, she doesn't know what to do with me. She doesn't know where I came from. No one does. So she sits far away from me, in all the rooms, when I'm a boy. Kay. But she would tell me stories. My yiayia would tell me a story about this lady, this crying lady in a purple hat. She said that if I ever saw a lady in a purple hat, not to go near this lady. She said this lady would try to take me away. I asked my yiayia why would she take me away? My yiayia didn't know. I asked why was she wearing a purple hat? My yiayia didn't know. *Just don't go near her. Don't let her get too close. She'll take you away.*

And I thought this woman was just a story.

But one day I saw. I saw a lady in a purple hat, at the water. Far away but getting closer. Shouting at me. I ran home, fast.

BASIL. And I started to see her *everywhere*. No matter where we went. Maybe she was *looking* for me. She walked around, in Thessaloniki. She walked around. And she wore too much make-up.

And she talked to herself. And she just, like, uh, she wore too much make-up. Smeared. You know? And always crying, muttering, far away. But getting closer. And me, always running home.

So that was real life. Kay? So then, forever I'm having this *dream*. This same *dream*. This nightmare. Almost every night.

PETER. Still?

BASIL. Almost every night. Still to this day.

PETER. Damn, so it's some shit you gotta work through.

BASIL. It is, it is some shit I gotta work through. So:

I'm standing in front of my house and there's Yiayia across the street, just my yiayia.

She's crossing slowly, crossing in this old-flowers dress. And I love her.

She gets to the big tree, and she leans against it. Suddenly I realize that she is dying, and I'm scared. I'm a little boy and I'm scared. And behind her the town is burning, or falling into the sea, or freezing up. This part is always different.

But my yiayia is leaning against the tree, and dying, and I can't move. I want to help her but I can't move. I'm afraid to run to help her. I'm afraid to touch her.

I feel the door thick behind me, I feel it there – and I hate that she's dying, she's dying, and she sees me, and she cries to me, and she asks me to come help her.

But I don't.

And I want to yell at her GO AWAY.

But I don't.

And now – ah – she is in front of me.

And she is wearing a purple hat. And she is wearing too much make-up. And her face is not my yiayia's. And I can tell in her eyes, she wants to take me away.

And I am too close to the face, the face of the lady. And then we start to fuse. A sweaty forehead, lipstick teeth uhhhhh like you know like uhhhhhhhhhh breathing hard, her skin into mine, her bones become mine uhhh like you know what I mean like uhh uhh uhhhhhhhhhhhhhh hahaha and we're in love, we're having sex, laughing, weird, but laughing, hahahaha and also melting like uhhhhhhhhhhhhhh we have the same arms uhhhhh we have the same chest uhhh the same legs uhhhhh the same face, and I am her, I am her, going uhhhhhhhhhhhhhhh uhhhhhhhhhhhhhhhhhhhhhhhhhhhhhhhhhhhhhhhh

My spine breaks into a million pieces.

And then.

I'm on the ground. I feel an incredible heat, from inside me. I am the heat. Okay, and I see that it *was* my yiayia, that I am my yiayia, and I am dying, and I am on the ground, and I am looking at the little boy who's me, who's also dying, and saying he's sorry, saying *I'm sorry, I'm sorry.*

And the city is burning, or freezing up.

Okay.

Okay. I wake up.

PETER. Okay yeah, you wake up.

BASIL. So I fear that lady in the purple hat.

PETER. So do I, now.

BASIL. Yes.

PETER. Okay.

BASIL. Okay.

PETER. Yeah.

BASIL. But, I don't know. I don't know how to make this into a story. Dreams are kind of boring.

(*Pause.*)

Some snow.

PETER. Yeah. Boy, eh? Damn.

(*The wind roars.*)

Fucker. Fuck. Haha. Whatever. Fuck. People are weird. I'm weird. You're weird, Basil.

BASIL. I'm weird? I'm not weird.

PETER. Fuck you. Ridiculous. I don't think I've had a cool dream like that in like fifteen years. When I sleep it's just dark noise pushing hard against my brain and teeth.

BASIL. Are you still feeling sadness?

PETER. Of course. It's fucking everywhere.

BASIL. Why do you look for it everywhere? You are looking for it and so you are finding it.

PETER. Okay then. I fucking hate myself.

BASIL. What – Peter –

PETER. Ah, fuck it. Funny times up here in the,

(*He wipes his nose.*)

in the truck.

(*Now:*)

(*Maiworm's bed.* **BASIL** *is going down on* **MAIWORM**. *That happens for a while and it's* *nice. Then it's done. They sit up, a little too formally.)*

MAIWORM. Thanks for going down on me, Basil.

BASIL. No problem, Maiworm.

(Pause. Re: the cunnilingus:)

Yeh it's funny I love that. Doing that.

MAIWORM. Amazing. Such amazing quality of yours.

BASIL. Haha. Yeh. But. Anyway.

MAIWORM. What was I going to say, earlier?

BASIL. I don't know.

MAIWORM. Darn, what was it.

(They're facing away from each other. Both staring off into space. **BASIL** *turns back to her.)*

BASIL. It's very nice, Maiworm, that you visit us in the mornings, even though your offices moved farther away.

MAIWORM. It's on the way.

BASIL. It's nice of you. How's your heart?

MAIWORM. My heart?

BASIL. Yeh.

MAIWORM. Physically?

BASIL. No. I like you so much.

*(***MAIWORM*** turns away.)*

MAIWORM. Um, oh, I remember what I was gonna say.

BASIL. Oh yeh?

MAIWORM. Oh yeah so you know how every Mid-March I do a cruise? I save a little to do a cruise with Jane Jr.

BASIL. Oh yeh? Okay, I'm in.

MAIWORM. How did you know I was going to ask?

BASIL. I knew, I knew.

MAIWORM. But I haven't even told you where I want to go this year.

BASIL. Where?

MAIWORM. I want to do a Mediterranean cruise.

> *(Pause.)*

Because I want to get to know Greece. From which you are. I like you so much too. What do you think about that?

BASIL. I don't want to do that, okay?

MAIWORM. Oh.

BASIL. You will have fun, though.

MAIWORM. Maybe it was a bad idea, anyway. Because we work together. Maybe that makes it a bad idea.

BASIL. Thessaloniki is not on the Mediterranean. It's on the Aegean.

MAIWORM. Oh, shoot. Well I think the boat scoops up into the Aegean. I think "Mediterranean" is just the headline.

BASIL. I don't want to behold my fuckup fuckoff past from a boat. Okay?

MAIWORM. Oh. Okay.

BASIL. Okay, that's great.

MAIWORM. Okay. Well.

> *(Pause.)*

I was also thinking about doing that Caribbean cruise again that I liked so much.

BASIL. Oh! Great. I'll easily do that with you and Jane Jr., yes!

MAIWORM. Okay, great. That's great. I was so worried there for a second. My brain was like a baked potato.

BASIL. Don't worry. Listen. I had a secret I was meaning to tell you.

MAIWORM. Uh-oh, okay. About your f-up f-off past?

BASIL. Oh. No. Nevermind.

MAIWORM. No. What is it?

BASIL. Nothing. Peter is so sad.

MAIWORM. Uh-oh. Really?

BASIL. I worry about him, and maybe we both should.

MAIWORM. How sad? More than usual?

BASIL. He's so curious about death. He's not with me, anymore, when he's with me.

(*They hear* **JANE JR.** *out in the kitchen.*)

Uh-oh, I'll sneak out. I'll see you at the warehouse?

MAIWORM. Yes, I'll check in with him. Thanks for telling me. Don't freeze out there. Good morning.

(**BASIL** *kisses* **MAIWORM** *on the forehead and then leaves.* **MAIWORM** *starts dressing for work.* **JANE JR.** *enters.*)

JANE JR. Mom. We have to talk about dark energy.

MAIWORM. Okay. Good morning.

JANE JR. An old scientist at the nursing home told me that we only know about 4% of the energy in the universe. Dark energy is everything else. So that freaks me out but not because of the universe out there, but because of the universe right here. Like if 96% of everything is unknown, does that mean that everything we *know* about is *also* 96% unknown? Like do we only know 4% about toenails? And so why am I so wrapped up in my problems?

MAIWORM. Yeah.

JANE JR. You know?

MAIWORM. Yeah.

JANE JR. It's hard because I know exactly what would solve all my problems. I just want to marry a famous singer. And I want to live with the famous singer in a warm place.

MAIWORM. Yeah, you've mentioned this before. Do you think that's an actionable goal?

JANE JR. I need your support on this.

MAIWORM. Well – what singer do you want to marry?

JANE JR. This one singer named Guadalupe X maybe. Honestly I have a list.

MAIWORM. Well – I guess before you marry Guadalupe X you have to get to know Guadalupe X, and before you get to know Guadalupe X you have to meet Guadalupe X.

JANE JR. Right.

MAIWORM. So you could go to their concerts, right? When they come through to Chicago or Milwaukee. Try to meet them after.

JANE JR. Incredibly low odds of that.

MAIWORM. So I don't know. Send a message on Twitter or Facebook.

JANE JR. They get 6,000 per day. How do I rise from the dreck? Can we think for a second about how one rises from the dreck?

MAIWORM. Okay, let's think.

(They sit there and think.)

Hey. It's getting late. I should go to the office. Someone from Davenport's coming to talk about heated permeable pavers. Remember my little dream?

JANE JR. Can we solve one problem at a time, please?

MAIWORM. No, I have to go.

JANE JR. Okay fine.

MAIWORM. Are you going to the nursing home today?

JANE JR. No.

MAIWORM. Why not?

JANE JR. It's too insane out there. Five minutes out there and your cheek skin gets frostbite.

MAIWORM. Yeah but I think you should *do* something today.

JANE JR. I have something to do tomorrow, but I don't have anything to do today.

MAIWORM. What do you have to do tomorrow?

JANE JR. Teach myself a dance.

MAIWORM. What dance?

JANE JR. This dance by Guadalupe X.

MAIWORM. What's it for?

JANE JR. Just for myself to know.

MAIWORM. Why don't you do it today?

JANE JR. Because today's not the day I do it. Today's just a day. And I have to get through it.

JANE JR. & MAIWORM. That rhymed.

MAIWORM. I have an idea.

*(**MAIWORM** hands **JANE JR.** a book.)*

JANE JR. *The Death and Life of Great American Cities.* By Jane Jacobs.

MAIWORM. It's so good. It's by Jane Jacobs.

JANE JR. This isn't my thing at all.

MAIWORM. It's my whole thing. She's very readable. She's iconic. She was an amazing woman – no college degree, a journalist, a mom, taking on these powerful, greedy men who were trying to put a highway through Greenwich Village. She organized a movement and she beat them! She wanted neighborhoods, eyes on the street, parks, strangeness, community, love, mess. I love her. And it's easy to lose sight of her in Evanston with our 37 subcommittees.

JANE JR. Is she why Evanston doesn't have a highway going through it?

MAIWORM. I think, yeah! I think this book might have given them the strength to resist that.

JANE JR. So that's why it takes so long to get to the airport.

MAIWORM. Hahaha, yep. Alright. Stay warm, stay cozy. You can eat the leftovers from Lucky Platter. Stay warm, stay cozy. Be a bean.

JANE JR. Okay.

(**MAIWORM** *heads out.*)

Oh fuck. MOM!!!!!!!!!!!!!!!!!!!!!!!

(**MAIWORM** *comes back.* **JANE JR.** *falls onto the ground.*)

MAIWORM. What happened?

JANE JR. I just got so scared. I was thinking about how lucky dad was to die when he did, because all the coasts will flood, and Florida won't exist, and New York won't exist, and an earthquake will hit the Pacific Northwest, so

Seattle and Oregon won't exist, and everyone will come to Evanston. Everyone will come to Evanston, Mom, and we'll look out our window and there will be thousands of people, all the time. And they'll all be so weird.

MAIWORM. Oh, dear. Oh, no. My brain went right to the burden on our infrastructure.

JANE JR. Let's leave Evanston. Let's live in Corpus Christi, Texas.

MAIWORM. Why?

JANE JR. It's falling into the sea!

MAIWORM. You want to fall into the sea?

JANE JR. Maybe just to get it over with!

MAIWORM. This is our home.

JANE JR. But there's something wrong! There's something under everything and it's making us all want to die! It's pushing out from under everything and it's telling us to die and you can't leave me alone with it.

MAIWORM. To die?

(**JANE JR.** *nods.* **MAIWORM** *sighs.*)

Do you want to come into work with me?

JANE JR. No.

MAIWORM. Alright then, you'll just have to figure out your day.

JANE JR. No kidding.

MAIWORM. I'm sorry I don't know what to say about the thing under everything that wants us to die.

JANE JR. It's fine.

MAIWORM. I don't know what you want me to say, Jane Jr.! You're getting on my nerves!

JANE JR. I am?

MAIWORM. Yeah.

JANE JR. Okay.

MAIWORM. Yes and – sorry. I love you. Sorry. See you tonight. We'll – uh. We're gonna find a way forward. We will.

>(**MAIWORM** *leaves.* **JANE JR.** *picks up the book.*)

JANE JR. *The Death and Life and Life and Life and Life and Life and Life of Mediocre American Towns.* By Jane Jacobs.

>(*She throws the book. Then! The dark energy reveals itself to* **JANE JR.** *for a moment. She closes her eyes.*)

>(*Across town, in the break room,* **PETER** *sniffles into a cup of coffee, and the dark energy reveals itself to him, too. He drops the coffee. He digs his nails into his forehead.*)

>(**BASIL** *enters.*)

BASIL. Morning!

2015

(The break room. **PETER** *and* **BASIL** *are drinking coffee.* **BASIL** *is reading from a sheet of paper.)*

BASIL. "The next day, he got up early and went to work. While laying the stones down and pressing them into the earth, he thought of Reggie's gigantic arms, and planned his escape." The end.

PETER. I like it.

BASIL. Thanks.

PETER. Wait, that's how it ends?

BASIL. Yeh.

PETER. I like it.

BASIL. Thanks.

PETER. I like that one a lot.

BASIL. Yeh. Thanks.

PETER. Wha'd you do last night?

BASIL. My cats had diarrhea all over, both of them. And then the one-eyed one threw up on my feet. Then for a while, you know, for a pretty long time, I stood at my kitchen window and played with my dick.

PETER. Yeah. I feel that. Did I tell you about the garbage disposal?

BASIL. No.

PETER. The garbage disposal's spitting up chunks of – Basil, I want to kill my wife.

(Pause.)

BASIL. You want to murder her?

PETER. Yeah, and then murder myself.

BASIL. Oh no, what? Don't.

    (**MAIWORM** *enters.*)

MAIWORM. Listen to this. They wrote an article about us! "CHANGES MAY COME FOR NEXT SNOW SEASON IN EVANSTON. By Arthur Hyde…"

BASIL. R.I.P. Bill Agrigento.

MAIWORM. R.I.P. Bill Agrigento.

PETER. Who the fuck is Bill Agrigento?

MAIWORM. "Evanston officials said they hope to make changes to their snow-fighting approach this winter season, including employing graphics to get messages to citizens. Jane Maiworm –"

BASIL. Oh!

PETER. Maiworm over here.

MAIWORM. It's just me, so! No Jackie Thorstensen.

BASIL. OH!

PETER. Congratulations Maiworm.

MAIWORM. "…Jane Maiworm, the city's assistant public works director in charge of city snow removal operations, told aldermen that 2014 marked the fourth of the past five winters that Evanston has seen above-average totals. Predictions for next winter 'are more of the same,' she said. Overtime (That's you!!) costs ran $312,350 for this winter compared to $722,722 a year ago, Maiworm said. 'The price of salt was very expensive last year,' she said, adding that it went up $25 per ton, hiking the city's material spending from $456,470 to –"

PETER. Hold on, I gotta take this call. This number keeps calling me non-stop.

(He walks off.)

MAIWORM. Should I keep reading?

BASIL. Sure.

MAIWORM. Maybe he wants to hear it though.

BASIL. Yes, maybe he wants to hear it. How's your neck?

MAIWORM. Oh, it's getting a little better.

BASIL. Good. I'm sorry about how much I cried the other day, with your fingers in my mouth.

MAIWORM. Oh, that's completely fine.

BASIL. I was just so happy.

MAIWORM. Me too.

BASIL. Sometimes I feel guilty about our little happiness.

MAIWORM. Why? It's ours.

*(***PETER*** comes back in and looks at them.)*

"...hiking the city's material spending from..." oh, let's see, let's see... "The city's efforts to reduce salt use by combining calcium chloride with beet juice reduced costs somewhat in 2014, but also led to reduced efficacy, as evidenced by an increase in minor vehicular accidents at the end of last winter season. The city devoted an entire week last November to increasing community awareness around best practices during a major snowfall, which included an interactive tour from inside the new salt dome. Maiworm said another big change officials hope to make 'is communicating better with our public' on snow parking regulations and the snow route parking ban. In that regard, Maiworm said she would like to see the use of more graphics in signage, something that other communities use. She introduced a rendering that highlighted the city's odd-even parking rule in a graphic that featured different colors for 'odd' and 'even.' 'Perhaps this is a better way of communicating with people,' she said, noting that 'our residential plowing efforts work best when people move their cars' in compliance with the rules, allowing crews (THAT'S YOU!) to clean the streets off." The end.

BASIL. Ho ho...!

Maiworm here in the paper.

(They look at **PETER**.*)*

Congratulations Maiworm.

MAIWORM. Well it keeps me up at night when they're confused about the signs. It does.

BASIL. Right. Do you know what keeps me up at night? What do the little bunnies do in the winter?

MAIWORM. Oh yeah?

BASIL. Yeah, so many bunnies in Evanston, what do the bunnies do in the winter?

PETER. Fuck you.

MAIWORM. What, Peter?

PETER. Okay, okay. I'll just sit and then I'll stand.

(He sits down.)

MAIWORM. Sorry I read that article. Is that why you're mad?

*(***PETER** *laughs quietly to himself.)*

I thought you might want to hear it.

PETER. Why'd you think that?

MAIWORM. Because, because.

PETER. Because what?

MAIWORM. Because you're my colleagues and friends. Doesn't that seem valid?

PETER. No.

MAIWORM. Oh, I didn't know.

BASIL. It is valid.

PETER. No it's not.

BASIL. Yes it is.

MAIWORM. Yeah?

BASIL. Yeh yeh, don't worry, Maiworm. I get it. I liked it.

MAIWORM. It's just a nice morning, and I wanted to share it with you. That felt valid to me.

PETER. Won't be long for nice. Nice for long. It's bout to fucking vortex again.

MAIWORM. I know.

PETER. So yeah. What the fuck, and fuck you.

BASIL. Hey. Stop it, come on.

PETER. Damnit. Sorry I got so mean at you.

MAIWORM. Oh it's okay, I just, I just walked in here, hoping to just talk.

PETER. Yeah. Sorry. Fuck. Hahahaha.

BASIL. Hahaha.

PETER. They should write a thing about what's it like what's it gonna be like when the supervolcano underneath Wyoming erupts, and everyone had to move to Evanston, and what Evanston is gonna do with all the people when they come.

BASIL. No one wants to read that. That's too big for this paper.

MAIWORM. I agree.

BASIL. Too big too heavy.

MAIWORM. Too big exactly, too heavy. This article's a little more administrative which I think is cool.

PETER. I think the terror in your heart when you think about it all ending is good. Fuck I don't know. Because it's cold. It's –

MAIWORM. Hahahaha yep. Well. Local news is important. Uh-oh. You guys gotta hit the road in like four minutes.

(**MAIWORM** *exits.*)

PETER. My brain's doing a weird thing. It's not letting me stand up and do what I need to do.

BASIL. What do you need to do?

PETER. *(Almost laughing.)* You're not gonna believe this.

BASIL. Believe what?

PETER. My wife was in an accident.

BASIL. What?

PETER. Just, fuckin...skidded off the road.

BASIL. When?

PETER. *(Almost laughing.)* This morning. Just now. She's in a coma.

(*Pause.*)

BASIL. Fuck you

PETER. No fuck you

BASIL. Fuck you

PETER. No fuck you

BASIL. Fuck you haha

PETER. No fuck you.

(*Pause.*)

BASIL. What?

PETER. What?

BASIL. Fuck you

PETER. No fuck you

BASIL. Fuck you haha

PETER. No fuck you.

BASIL. What the fuck is going on?

PETER. I just feel bad because I was hating her real bad, real bad today worse than everything. I just couldn't stand to look at her. Can't stand to hear her voice. She's been such a big disappointment to me. I mean I love her, but I was thinking: *I'm gonna kill you motherfucker I'm gonna fuck you up*. What a bad thing to think to myself. But also, just a dumb thought to myself. Because I was tired. And really, I do like her, a lot. And think about how much I've liked her – so much. I've liked her so much more than I haven't liked her. In terms of time. Just that nice comfort of all that time. Of liking her all that time.

BASIL. Peter – she's in a coma?

PETER. She skidded off the road.

BASIL. And you are frozen.

PETER. Yeah, I am.

BASIL. Peter.

PETER. Hahahaha.

BASIL. Peter, you should go to the hospital, I think.

PETER. What?

BASIL. Go see your wife in the hospital. Right now.

PETER. No I mean that makes sense.

BASIL. I can drive you.

PETER. True true true true true.

BASIL. Let's go.

PETER. No. Thanks for trying to help but it takes a while to sink in. My toes are cold.

BASIL. We have to leave.

PETER. Negative thirteen. Butta time. Suppa time for us. Butta time.

    (**MAIWORM** *enters.*)

MAIWORM. Peter. I just got a phone call from the hospital. From my friend Hannah at the hospital.

PETER. Okay.

MAIWORM. She said you hung up. Um, have you heard the news?

PETER. Yeah. There's something in this room. It's not letting me stand up.

    (**BASIL** *goes over and helps* **PETER** *stand up.*)

BASIL. Let's all go over to the hospital.

MAIWORM. Yeah.

BASIL. Let's go Peter, yeh?

PETER. Sure. They should write an article about what it was like.

BASIL. What what was like?

PETER. When you got me to stand up.

    (*They head out.*)

    (*Now:*)

(**BASIL** *drives the salt truck alone. He's listening to a country song.* He turns off the song. In the silence, we dip into a view of his bottomless sadness. We shouldn't have access to this.*)

(*A thud. He gets out to check the chute. When he's outside, he sees the* **LADY IN THE PURPLE HAT** *crossing the road. She's muttering to herself. He stares at her until she's gone.*)

(*Now:*)

(**JANE JR.** *is dancing to a pop song by Guadalupe X.* She dances very hard. The dance is sensual. The song sounds like it was created by a deep-sea creature.* **JANE JR.** *messes up and screams.*)

(**MAIWORM** *enters.* **JANE JR.** *turns off the stereo.*)

JANE JR. Hi. Okay. Wow, I'm sweating.

MAIWORM. You were dancing.

JANE JR. Yeah, it's that dance by Guadalupe X. Yeah but it's not finished.

MAIWORM. Amazing though.

JANE JR. Well it took me a year to get around to it.

MAIWORM. It's great that you dance. It's a great thing about you!

JANE JR. Thanks.

---

* A license to produce *EVANSTON SALT COSTS CLIMBING* does not include a performance license for any third-party or copyrighted music. Licensees should create an original composition or use music in the public domain. For further information, please see the Music and Third-Party Materials Use Note on page iii.

MAIWORM. You can keep dancing right now.

JANE JR. No, I'm fine.

MAIWORM. You don't like dancing around me.

JANE JR. Not really.

MAIWORM. Oh. I wish you did. I wish very much that you did.

JANE JR. I'm sorry, Mom. How was your day?

MAIWORM. It was fine. It was a day. I hated it.

JANE JR. I'm sorry.

MAIWORM. Not your fault.

JANE JR. Right, not my fault. So funny that I do that. "Don't say sorry if it's not your fault."

MAIWORM. It's okay.

JANE JR. I know.

MAIWORM. Can I tell you about my day? And then I want you to tell me about yours.

JANE JR. Yes, that's fine.

MAIWORM. That's a plan.

JANE JR. Let's shake on it.

(They shake on it.)

Good. Good handshake.

MAIWORM. Good handshake. So I went to work today and Jackie slapped me on the back and ohhhh

Oops

It's my anxiety, one sec.

Yeah. Yup. Anyway

(She quietly panics.)

JANE JR. Mom, mom, mom.

(**MAIWORM** *manages to breathe.*)

MAIWORM. Sorry, it's just... Peter's wife died.

JANE JR. What? How?

MAIWORM. I told you she was in a coma.

JANE JR. No you didn't! When? I haven't seen you very much. What happened?

MAIWORM. I could have sworn I told you. The road was icy and she skidded into ongoing traffic. Ongoing? Oncoming. Traffic. She was in a coma this whole past week. And she slipped away this morning. Their daughter was in the back seat and thank God the daughter is alive.

JANE JR. How old's the daughter?

MAIWORM. Six. And oh my God, it's so horrible, and Peter is just...

And I have been feeling this guilt.

JANE JR. What? It's not your fault.

MAIWORM. But why wasn't that road salted? Or salted enough?

JANE JR. Mom you're not the salter.

MAIWORM. We're going to go forward with them, the heated, the heated permeable

But we'd have to outsource, we'd have to outsource all the

(*Panic.*)

I was looking for solutions. And of course.

Heated permeable pavers

(*Panic.*)

MAIWORM. And his wife

And then what, I fire him?

JANE JR. Mom. Um.

Mom. Um.

Shhh. Um.

You're going to be okay. Everything's okay.

You're home now, you're...cozy.

MAIWORM. Okay.

JANE JR. Tell me you're cozy.

MAIWORM. I am cozy. And I asked her what that would do to the budget...

JANE JR. Who?

MAIWORM. Jackie Thorstensen.

JANE JR. We don't have to talk about work.

MAIWORM. ...and she showed me the budget, Jane Jr., and my God, the cost. Oh, God.

Heated

Permeable

Pavers

No one knows how to

Put them

In

We'd have to hire a company.

They'd have all their own people –

All their own

All their own guys.

But there is *so* much good about them. So much *good* about them.

What am I going to tell the boys?

JANE JR. Tell them everything's gonna be okay. That's it. That's all. Start with that.

MAIWORM. Yeah. Yes. Okay. Yes.

(**MAIWORM** *lies down. Panic.*)

could be heated by solar power, could be hooked up to a central electric grid –

I mean they ain't kidding, team, it's up to seventy degrees –

bioswales are being – gonna make a ton of difference from a gas perspective –

gonna make a ton of difference from a SALT perspective –

JANE JR. Mom...

MAIWORM. so much to, so – proposals and grants – subsections – is it even financially viable to make all streets heated – and Jane Jacobs wouldn't – or Jane Jacobs would – yes on the street – messier, she'd want it – messier – I'm a disgrace, all our roads hollowed out and empty – delivery trucks and parking garages – no public sphere – she'd hate me – no – a road can be fixed – what do we do? just let sinkholes – where'd I get my officious little soul –

JANE JR. Mom!

MAIWORM. And the salt companies? The salt companies? And the labor –! Well in Davenport they've developed a mechanism to lay brick streets, it's like this big slanted platform and as you back up it just slides the bricks into place, that would also work for a permeable brick, so Evanston could in effect put these streets in themselves through public works employees...

MAIWORM. maybe so maybe so maybe I'll fight for that –

Sorry, sorry... Jane Jr., I'm sorry. I'm here. I'm present.

JANE JR. It's so frustrating when you bring home your work like that.

MAIWORM. I know.

JANE JR. I just wish that you weren't the Assistant Director of Public Works. I wish you were the Assistant Director of *Private* Works.

MAIWORM. I wish I were the *Director* of Private Works.

JANE JR. I'm sorry about Peter's wife.

MAIWORM. I know.

JANE JR. I love you.

(Pause.)

My day was pretty good.

MAIWORM. Oh God, yes, your day.

JANE JR. My day was pretty bad. Well, I took the bus to go volunteer at the nursing home yay. And the old scientist was telling me about how *Homo sapiens* have been destroying the earth from the beginning, that's just what we do, we destroy, even farmers and hunter-gatherers in the Amazon et cetera. And then I was singing "Angel from Montgomery," John Prine version, for the old scientist and he peed without knowing it and the pee was traveling really slowly towards me.

MAIWORM. The pee was traveling towards you?

JANE JR. Yes. Really slowly towards me across the floor.

MAIWORM. Is it okay if I laugh?

JANE JR. No.

MAIWORM. Hahahaha.

JANE JR. Hahaha. So um, your birthday is coming up huh.

MAIWORM. Oh right. I completely forgot.

JANE JR. So hey what do you want for your birthday?

MAIWORM. Oh I don't know. You don't have to get me anything.

JANE JR. I want to.

MAIWORM. Jeez. Chocolate vodka? One of those big bouncy balls that you sit on instead of a chair? Who knows.

JANE JR. Okay thanks because I just want you to have a good birthday this year because you've been working so hard and you need to know that you are loved and appreciated and stuff like that. And one of my intentions for this year is being a better daughter to you but also a better *friend* to you –

(**MAIWORM** *is putting her big coat back on.*)

Why are you putting that coat back on?

MAIWORM. Oh I just, I have to run back to the office real quick.

JANE JR. You do?

MAIWORM. Yes – I just have to run back real quick. I need the database.

JANE JR. Mom.

MAIWORM. I just, I need the database.

(*The Guadalupe X song suddenly blares on.*[*] **JANE JR.** *screams.*)

---

[*] A license to produce *EVANSTON SALT COSTS CLIMBING* does not include a performance license for any third-party or copyrighted music. Licensees should create an original composition or use music in the public domain. For further information, please see the Music and Third-Party Materials Use Note on page iii.

(*Now:*)

(**MAIWORM** *runs into* **PETER** *outside the warehouse.*)

PETER. Hey, Maiworm.

MAIWORM. Oh my God, Peter. What are you doing here?

PETER. It's my job. What are you doing here?

MAIWORM. Well I'm just – I had to – Oh Peter. How are you doing?

PETER. Yeah I'm alright. Had a dream last night that I was getting back in the truck. Was climbing up the driver's side but the door never came. I was climbing up forever. It was the tallest truck in the world. I told my daughter. She's writing a story about it. Been a while since I had a cool dream like that.

MAIWORM. Okay. Yes. Oh, Peter.

PETER. Oh, what?

MAIWORM. Alright. Well, listen Peter, I'm so sorry, and if there's anything, anything at all I can –

PETER. There's Basil's car. See ya Maiworm.

MAIWORM. Did you get my stew?

PETER. Yeah. My daughter's a picky eater. We mostly do Domino's. Followed by Oreos. Yeah my belly's jiggling all day with Domino's. Yeah. Fuck. I been to hell and back with Domino's.

(*Now:*)

(*The salt truck. Music loud.*)

---

* A license to produce *EVANSTON SALT COSTS CLIMBING* does not include a performance license for any third-party or copyrighted music. Licensees should create an original composition or use music in the public domain. For further information, please see the Music and Third-Party Materials Use Note on page iii.

PETER. Good to see you again.

BASIL. Likewise brother.

PETER. Longest week of my life. I had to get back in the truck. Yeah I saw the weather forecast and all her family's been around all the fucking time and I can't stand them so when I saw the weather forecast I just fucking called in and was like: I just have to get back in the truck.

BASIL. Right. Well if you want me to drive or anything.

PETER. No I'm good. Hoo hoo hoo. This is a big one. Ooo, hoo hoo, fuck.

BASIL. Yep, heh heh

PETER. Hoo hoo

BASIL. You been eating?

PETER. Yeah, you?

BASIL. Of course, I love eating. How's um, how's the

(**BASIL** *turns the music down.*)

How's your daughter?

PETER. She's okay, she's okay. She's, uh. To be perfectly honest, I ordered Domino's like three or four times this week. Me and my daughter are like obsessed with it. The medium pan pizza. It's fucking great. We just sit there and watch the pizza tracker.

BASIL. What's the pizza tracker?

PETER. It's a thing on Dominos.com that shows you when they put it in the oven, and when it's out for delivery. It's like a thermometer going long this way, and it just has this red pulse for the different stages of the pizza. We just sit there and watch that.

BASIL. Uh-huh. And how's the, uh, funeral preparation, is that, do you need –

PETER. You heard about that thing about how Nutella can cause cancer?

BASIL. No.

PETER. Oh everyone's saying Nutella can cause cancer.

BASIL. Oh.

PETER. You haven't heard this? It's in all the tweets. And all the articles about the tweets, know what I mean?

BASIL. No I don't. That's sad. I love Nutella.

PETER. Yeah. It's cuz of the palm oil. Cuz apparently palm oil, when you heat it up, it's cancer. And there's a ton of palm oil in Nutella. But who knew that? They didn't know it caused cancer. How could they know that? It's not anything Ferrero did wrong. Ferrero's the company that makes Nutella. I know that cuz my brother-in-law works there. But now all the stores are all pulling Nutella off all the shelves. Yeah it's crazy when I saw the news, I was like, "my brother-in-law works for Ferrero." He sells Nutella to Wal-Mart. He goes down to Arkansas and sells Nutella directly to the Wal-Mart family. They're scared. My brother-in-law. And his friends at the office. The office in New Jersey. They're just people. They see the news on the internet. They drive to work the next day. They're all like: "Oh no – look at this news story. It's about us." "Fuck. I'm gonna kill myself." "Hey, good morning everyone." "Oh hey Gary." "Did you hear the news?" "Yeah we did Gary. Fuck." "I'm so sorry, Gary." "Me too, Francine." "I'm gonna kill myself." "Yeah, just do it, just kill yourself." "No, don't. We'll get through this somehow." "Yeah. Don't worry." "We're all in this together." "I love you." "Fuck don't say you love me." "Why?" "Cuz it hurts, it hurts to love you, it hurts to love all you people." "Fuck." Fuck. One little tweet and suddenly Nutella means cancer. You start to understand why oil companies and, you know, gun people, plastic people, pharmacy people and whatever, fight back. Why they try to stay on top. Cuz they're just people. And they all want to kill themselves.

BASIL. All of them?

PETER. Yeah.

BASIL. Why do they all want to kill themselves?

PETER. Because the world doesn't need us. Not one little bit. It would be better for the world if we all killed ourselves. The planet would thank us. And we all know it.

(He points out the window.)

See, there's my house. Way too many cars. Way too many people.

BASIL. How are you?

PETER. I truck in the summers, you know that right?

BASIL. Of course I do.

PETER. I'll have to figure out what to do with my daughter this summer. Fuck.

BASIL. Well maybe you can stay here and do the summer work with me.

PETER. Fuck no. Don't you hate the summer work?

BASIL. I do, I do hate the summer work. It is so hot, fixing the hot roads.

PETER. Yeah fuck no. Plus I got my summer friends. You know Jason from Montana? All the guys that do trucking around here, all those guys are from Montana. Those Montana boys, I love 'em. Especially Jason.

BASIL. Cool.

PETER. "If I can't truck it, fuck it," that's what his business card says.

BASIL. Peter...

PETER. Yeah?

BASIL. Tell me. Tell me if you want to talk.

PETER. We're talking.

BASIL. About what happened. Just tell me. And I am here.

PETER. Sure.

> (*Far away, the* **LADY IN THE PURPLE HAT**.)

BASIL. Peter...

PETER. Yeah?

BASIL. Do you see that lady?

> (*The truck skids for a moment. Then steadies.*)

PETER. Shit. Sorry. Fuck. You know what? That was the same spot, the stretch where my wife – fuck, hold up, I'm gonna back up.

> (*The sound of a truck backing up. He pulls a lever.*)

I'm gonna –

> (*He dumps a lot of salt on the road. Too much salt. A white mound. He gets out of the truck and spreads it out on the ground. Takes a while. His boots on that salt.*)

> (*Now:*)

> (*The house.* **JANE JR**. *and* **BASIL**.)

JANE JR. Thanks for checking your email. She's at work, so I thought right now would be a good time.

BASIL. Great time. Just finished my shift. So what's your secret plan?

JANE JR. Okay I was thinking about throwing my mom a surprise party. For her birthday.

BASIL. That sounds like a good plan.

JANE JR. Great. I've never thrown a surprise party.

BASIL. I've thrown seven.

JANE JR. Oh good, oh great. Who should we invite?

BASIL. Well. Peter...

Hank.

Hannah.

Hiro.

HJ.

JIM!

Parker.

Greg.

Dave & Deb.

Didi.

Wally Bobkiewicz.

Jackie?

JANE JR. Totally. Wait. Hold on. Maybe we shouldn't do this. It's freaking me out. Too many details.

BASIL. Oh okay.

JANE JR. Let's small talk. Tell me how you are.

BASIL. I'm okay. Stuff, these days, has been a little rough.

JANE JR. Well maybe we should push through and do the surprise party anyway. As an optimistic act.

BASIL. Maybe so.

JANE JR. Maybe um. Maybe it could involve alcohol.

BASIL. That's perfect.

JANE JR. Doesn't she like that bar?

BASIL. Which one?

JANE JR. That bar over there somewhere?

BASIL. The Celtic Knot?

JANE JR. *(Making his soft c a hard c.)* The Celtic Knot. Yeah.

BASIL. Yes, she loves it. She loves the fiddle players.

JANE JR. Okay good. Good. Blah. I dunno. Maybe it's not the right year to do this party.

BASIL. Oh.

JANE JR. Damn. I'm so annoying. Sorry.

BASIL. You're not annoying.

JANE JR. Change of subject, please.

BASIL. Okay. Why's your name Jane Jr.?

JANE JR. Because my mom's name is Jane.

BASIL. Who, Maiworm?

JANE JR. Yeah.

BASIL. But she's not your real mother.

JANE JR. Yes she is.

BASIL. Oh. I thought. Oh.

JANE JR. When she showed up, I was five, and her name was Jane too, so I crossed my arms and said "Well then I guess I'm Jane Jr.!" And we lived happily ever after. Change of subject please.

BASIL. How do you like being an American young woman?

JANE JR. Funny you should ask. I feel absolutely nothing about that.

BASIL. Oh.

JANE JR. That was a joke, okay. It's a terrible place. And it's gonna get worse. You're lucky you're not from here.

BASIL. But I'm here now. And it's nice to be a small man observing things in the new Rome. In the days before the fall. Hopefully I'll be alive to see the nasty emperors' bacchanals. And then – ah! I will feel the stones crack underneath my feet.

JANE JR. Oh. Okay cool. Okay cool. So, hey, I've been meaning to ask you...who *are* you?

BASIL. Who *am* I?

JANE JR. Sorry, that was rude.

BASIL. No it wasn't. I, um –

JANE JR. My mom giggles when your name comes up. And sometimes she sighs. Why didn't you come on that cruise with us last year? At the last minute?

BASIL. Oh. Well. My heart was doing a thing it does sometimes, which is where it violently rejects experiences where I might have to pretend to be happier than I am. And I'm usually a pretty happy guy! So I have to listen to my heart!

JANE JR. Okay but couldn't you just fake it for one *week*? She was so sad when you didn't come. And sometimes you just have to fake it for the people you care about. Sorry.

BASIL. Don't be sorry. You're probably right.

Oh.

Ah.

JANE JR. Are you okay? Sorry.

BASIL. Yes, I just touched a little sadness for a second. But I moved through it.

JANE JR. Why were you sad? Cuz of what I said? Sorry.

BASIL. Don't be sorry. I moved through it. I'm fine.

JANE JR. That fast? Weird. Look, I'm sorry if I made you sad for a second but it's also okay to be sad for a second.

BASIL. Right.

JANE JR. Look, I'm completely overwhelmed by having to live the rest of my life. I'm completely bored and terrified every second of every day. And I'm so so so – just – very very very lonely.

BASIL. Oh. Mm. Right right right. You're reminding me so much of. Nevermind. Listen, Jane Jr. It's as simple as. Hm. Well think of it this way: We're all just: Have you, uh... there's:

JANE JR. What is that? What are you doing? Are you trying to fix me?

BASIL. I don't know. Sorry. I feel a little confused.

(Weird pause. Shockingly long. **BASIL** *smiles.* **JANE JR.** *doesn't. She studies him.* **BASIL** *gets very uncomfortable. Eventually,* **BASIL** *giggles.)*

Ahm...

(He finds the book.)

Oh. *The Death and Life of Great American Cities*?

JANE JR. Yeah.

BASIL. Your mom asked us to read this, and none of us did. Have you read it?

JANE JR. Not yet. My mom wants me to.

BASIL. I skimmed it and memorized a quote so that she would think I read it:

"There is a quality even meaner
than outright ugliness or disorder,

and this meaner quality
is the dishonest mask of pretended order,
achieved by ignoring
or suppressing
the real order
that is struggling to exist
and to be served."

    (**JANE JR.** *goes to a dark place. Starts to cry.*)

Party? Yes or no?

JANE JR. It's so much pressure. I feel like this is one of those decisions, where I'll look back, and I'll either say: "I'm so fucking mad at myself for not throwing my mom that party." Or: "I'm so fucking mad at myself for throwing my mom such an embarrassing party where I embarrassed myself and my mom and everyone because it was awkward and poorly planned."

BASIL. What about the option where the party is good?

JANE JR. Oh, isn't Peter's wife's funeral soon?

BASIL. Yes, it's on Saturday.

JANE JR. Okay, that settles it. No party. Mom will just have a sad birthday this year. Out of respect.

BASIL. Okay great. That's great.

    (*Pause.*)

JANE JR. I guess we'll never be friends.

BASIL. What? Why not?

JANE JR. You're afraid to be sad in front of people.

    (*The door suddenly blows open.*)

BASIL. Wow!

2016

(The break room. **PETER** *and* **BASIL**. *Behind them, there's no salt. They're holding their coffee.* **PETER** *has a boot on his leg.* **BASIL** *hands* **PETER** *his phone.)*

PETER. What's this?

BASIL. It's my story. On an online literary journal.

PETER. Wow, cool.

BASIL. It's a micro-fiction story. You can hold it in the palm of your hand. You can read it in under three minutes. You can read it right now.

PETER. Cool, wow. Cool font.

BASIL. Are you reading it?

PETER. No my eyes are all stupid. Can you send me the link?

BASIL. *(Taking the phone back.)* Sure.

PETER. Look at the boot on my leg.

BASIL. Yes I saw it. What happened to you?

PETER. I tried to drive into Lake Michigan.

BASIL. Oh no. What. Why?

PETER. I knew it wouldn't work. Cuz of the frozen-ness of the lake. But you know that spot where Lee Street ends? The path just rolls right down into the water. Hit the ice and spun out. Just wanted to feel it for a second.

BASIL. Feel what.

PETER. Like maybe it could happen.

BASIL. What could happen.

PETER. Death could happen.

BASIL. Death could always happen.

PETER. Well maybe it *should* happen.

BASIL. But you've got your daughter.

PETER. Yeah, fuck, Basil! I know I've got my daughter.

BASIL. Oh, Peter.

PETER. Fucked up my tibia. Anyway, I did something. I tried something. No matter what you say, I'm a little proud of myself.

(*Pause.*)

BASIL. Where's all the salt?

(**MAIWORM** *enters with* **JANE JR.**)

Maiworm, where's all the salt? Oh, hi, Jane Jr.

JANE JR. Hey.

BASIL. What are you doing here?

JANE JR. My mom made me come in with her. I was spinning out.

BASIL. Right.

PETER. Hi, Jane Jr.

JANE JR. Hey. Sorry about your life.

PETER. What?

MAIWORM. So, um. Some big news I wanted to tell you.

BASIL. Oh yeah?

PETER. What's that?

MAIWORM. (*It's her anxiety.*) Yeah – oops.

It's my – one sec.

(**MAIWORM** *reveals a piece of paper.*)

MAIWORM. Okay. Sorry about that. This is, uh, from the Department of Environmental Services. And, uh. Everything's gonna be okay.

(She starts to read with the seriousness of a eulogy.)

"Despite its many miraculous uses throughout human history, and due to its unique chemical structure, salt spells disaster for the soil in which it infiltrates. Through ion exchange, the Sodium ion lodges within the soil and releases other ions such as Calcium, Magnesium, and Potassium into the groundwater as well as increasing metal mobilization. This causes depletion in the soil, and changes the soil permeability, causing the soil to become impervious, which blocks water infiltration, reduces soil stability, and decreases the soil pH and overall fertility. Salt can have impacts on soil biota, soil welling and crusting, soil electrical conductivity, soil osmotic potential, soil dispersion, and structural stability. Salt kills the grass, shrubs, and foliage along the roadside. Salt primarily causes dehydration which leads to foliage damage but also causes osmotic stress that harms root growth. Salt can lead to plant death and can also cause a colonization of salt tolerant species, such as cattails, thereby reducing species diversity. Salt severely damages health of wildlife, including birds and mammals. Birds, the most sensitive wildlife species to salt, often mistake road salt crystals for seeds or grit, resulting in toxicosis and..."

(She suddenly lets out a loud sob.)

JANE JR. Keep reading, Mom.

MAIWORM. Okay. "...resulting in toxicosis and death. Wildlife such as deer and rabbits are also attracted to the roadway to ingest salt crystals, which leads to higher incidents of vehicular accidents. Particularly high concentrations of Sodium and Chloride can be found in snow melt, which many animals drink to relieve thirst and potentially can cause salt toxicity including dehydration, confusion, and death." The end. So that's what happens to bunnies in the winter. They eat salt and die confused.

BASIL. Oh.

(**MAIWORM** *crumples the paper into a ball.*)

MAIWORM. And, you know, it's my own way of telling you – with some science, why...ummm.

BASIL. You can tell us.

PETER. What's happening here.

JANE JR. You can do it, Mom.

MAIWORM. Everything's gonna be okay. Have you two ever heard of heated permeable pavers?

PETER. No.

BASIL. Yes.

MAIWORM. What do you know about them?

BASIL. Expensive.

MAIWORM. Yes. And they're, uh, gonna displace you. They're gonna make your jobs obsolete.

BASIL. What are you saying, Maiworm?

MAIWORM. They wouldn't let me hire you for –

(**PETER** *coughs.*)

PETER. This fuckin cough, terrible.

BASIL. Sorry, Maiworm, didn't catch that.

MAIWORM. They're objectively better. Sorry to say. They're safer. They're safer. And I fought for a whole year to get you guys trained to install them, but it just doesn't make sense. We have to bring in a company, hire a company, their team, to do it.

PETER. Maiworm, what are you saying? Are you firing us?

MAIWORM. No. I'm warning you.

PETER. What the fuck?

MAIWORM. Sorry. Everything's gonna be okay. What happened was – I spent all year doing the work that terrified me – which is learning everything about heated permeable pavers. And then I got a grant! From the best – from a major environmental foundation, to make it happen, here in Evanston, one block at a time! And the mayor gave me a little, uh, coin thing. And they fired Jackie who was stuck in her ways, and they made me Director.

JANE JR. Heck yeah!

BASIL. Ho ho!

MAIWORM. Director of Private Works.

BASIL. Amazing.

MAIWORM. I mean Public Works.

BASIL. Amazing.

MAIWORM. What am I gonna say, it's not nice? It's nice. But boys...big changes are coming. And in all the fury in my mind, I forgot to order the salt for right now. The salt for this moment, right now. So we don't have any salt. And new salt is on the way. The salt from Skokie. The guys from Skokie are gonna salt our roads today.

BASIL. Oh! The Skokie guys!

MAIWORM. But they use too much beet juice. So expect purplish roads this week.

PETER. So wait, lemme get this straight. Salt trucks have had their day in Evanston?

MAIWORM. It may indeed work out that way. I'm so sorry. I wanted to give you some warning, some time to look for new opportunities...

PETER. Oh shit.

BASIL. When is this happening?

MAIWORM. Well, not *today* –

JANE JR. OW! Sorry. I need to cut my toenails.

2017

PETER. Oh shit.

BASIL. When is this happening?

MAIWORM. Well, not *today* –

2018

PETER. Oh shit.

BASIL. When is this happening?

MAIWORM. Well, not *today* –

2019

PETER. Oh shit.

2020

BASIL. When is this –

2021

MAIWORM. Well, not –

2022

PETER. Oh –

20##

BASIL. When –

2###

MAIWORM. Well –

####

JANE JR. OW! Sorry. I need to cut my toenails.

2016

PETER. Yeah but are we actually talking about this? I've been working here for almost twenty years.

MAIWORM. I know! I'm sorry! Jesus Christ, I'm so sorry. This came out of love for you, Peter. For you. For your wife. I don't want that to happen again. I want to start a foundation for –

PETER. For what?

MAIWORM. For your wife, for that stretch of road. For road safety. A foundation. Maybe you could work at the foundation.

PETER. A foundation for a stretch of road where one woman died?

MAIWORM. Yes, I really think that could make a difference –

PETER. Not only that, she died because her husband didn't salt the road good enough.

MAIWORM. Peter, no...

BASIL. No, Peter.

PETER. Why Evanston, that's my question.

MAIWORM. What?

PETER. Why does Evanston have to be the one?

MAIWORM. Not the only one, and I'll tell you why, because –

PETER. Tell me why –

MAIWORM. Well Peter we're a very green city, we were voted – we have – a duty, a reputation, for sustainability.

PETER. See I wondered if you'd say that. That green shit. I'm not making the world any less green than the next guy. And the green shit is probably gonna kill us too. We're humans, we fuck up and die. So what. And I have a reputation as a salt truck guy. And I like that reputation. It's one of the only things I have that I like. Why can't we let anything just fucking *be* –

(*Something shifts in the room.*)

This fucking room. Does anyone else feel that?

JANE JR. Yeah.

PETER. There's something in the fucking room.

JANE JR. Yeah, there's something underneath everything.

MAIWORM. I feel it.

JANE JR. You do?

MAIWORM. It's horrible.

I probably brought it in!

PETER. You didn't bring it in. That shit's been here.

(*Suddenly,* **MAIWORM** *gasps.*)

MAIWORM. What did you just say, Basil?

BASIL. What? I didn't say anything. That was Peter.

MAIWORM. No, you just yelled at me. You just screamed at me to Go Away.

BASIL. I did? No I didn't.

MAIWORM. I'm sorry. I'm so sorry!

(**MAIWORM** *runs out of the room.*)

BASIL. Did I yell that?

PETER. No.

JANE JR. No. She left her coat! Mom!

(*She runs after* **MAIWORM**.)

PETER. Fuck. Fuck. Why'd she come in here just to make us feel dread? FUCK!

BASIL. Ah, yeh.

PETER. Fuck. Fuck. You wanna come over for dinner?

BASIL. Sure. Thank you.

PETER. I gotta clean up then! Fuck! It's okay. My daughter and I, we've been trying to, um. Make a game out of it.

BASIL. Should I come over at six?

PETER. Yeah come over at six and we'll talk this shit out.

BASIL. Okay. I should go see if Maiworm is okay. I didn't tell her to Go Away, did I? I've been sleeping with her for three years.

PETER. I know.

BASIL. Oh!

(**BASIL** *starts to leave.*)

PETER. Hey why didn't you tell me? It made me sad when you wouldn't talk to me like that.

BASIL. Really?

PETER. Yeah. I never knew what the fuck was going on with you except in your dreams and stories.

BASIL. Really?

PETER. Yeah. You live alone, you diddle your dick, you could die alone and no one would know. And I feel like that's how you prefer it and honestly it makes me sad.

BASIL. Well I got so sad when you started hanging out with the Montana boys more than me. Why did you stop being my only friend?

PETER. The fuck?

BASIL. I don't know.

PETER. I don't know. You make me laugh but you don't make me feel better. And you never asked me how I was doing, when my wife died.

BASIL. Yes I did.

PETER. No you didn't.

BASIL. Yes, I did, all the time.

PETER. Well it felt like you didn't really want to know.

BASIL. It felt that way?

PETER. Yeah, it did.

BASIL. Well that is very strange to me.

PETER. Yeah.

BASIL. You wanted me to go down into the feeling with you? I didn't know if I should. Should I go down into it now? I will go down into it now, for you, Peter, if that's what you want.

PETER. No don't do it *now*.

BASIL. You needed it then and I didn't do it. Maybe I was scared.

PETER. Oh *you* were scared?

BASIL. I'm scared. You are scaring me.

You are finding me out, Peter. I tell everyone I don't feel it, but I feel it.

I wake up every night with my own hands choking me to death.

In the morning I pretend I moved through it.

But I never move through it.

And I'm scared. I feel like a little boy.

PETER. Why?

BASIL. Because I'm – I'm – oh no.

PETER. What?

BASIL. I don't know, I don't know.

PETER. Are you okay?

(**BASIL** *finds the door behind him.*)

BASIL. Oh, is this happening?

PETER. Why are you looking at me like that?

BASIL. There are new things that can be done.

(**BASIL** *leaves.*)

PETER. What the fuck, Basil? Fuck. It's fucking hot in here all a sudden.

(*Now:*)

(*The wind roars.* **MAIWORM** *is walking through the polar vortex. She pushes against the wind.* **JANE JR.** *runs out and finds her.*)

JANE JR. Mom, what are you doing? You left your coat! How am I gonna get home?

(**MAIWORM** *gives her the car key.*)

MAIWORM. Here's the car key. You head home. I'll walk to work.

JANE JR. But it's so cold!

MAIWORM. Jane Jr., is this what you've been living with?

JANE JR. What?

MAIWORM. Is this what it feels like? I didn't know!

JANE JR. What?

MAIWORM. I'm a horrible mother!

JANE JR. What?

MAIWORM. I'm a horrible mother!

JANE JR. WHAT?

MAIWORM. I'M A HORRIBLE STEP-MOTHER!!!

JANE JR. No you're not! Please don't say that! That makes me feel broken.

MAIWORM. What?

JANE JR. That makes me feel BROKEN!!

MAIWORM. What?

JANE JR. I JUST MISS YOU ALL THE TIME. EVEN WHEN I'M WITH YOU.

MAIWORM. I'M SORRY I CAN'T HEAR YOU – THIS WIND! GO HOME.

(**JANE JR.** *leaves.* **MAIWORM** *walks.*)

(*Now:*)

(**BASIL** *alone, walking in the storm. He's on his phone.*)

BASIL. Maiworm? Are you okay? Call me back!

(*He hangs up. His phone rings.*)

Hello?

(*Pause.*)

Yiayia?

(*Now:*)

(**JANE JR.** *alone with a bottle of chocolate vodka.*)

JANE JR. (*On the phone.*) Mom? Wally Bobkiewicz called and said you weren't at the office. Where are you?

(*She picks up the bottle.*)

I'm day-drinking some of your chocolate vodka. It's kind of bad and kind of good. I've gotta make changes this year. Like you, today, you made that change, and it was hard but you DID it. And I'm so proud of you. And I don't think you're a bad step-mom. You're my mom. And you're good. You're so good. And I think I'm just kind of a bad person. I'm bad at being a person. And I don't think I'll ever find someone. I don't think I'll ever find someone to battle the thing underneath everything, when it comes for us, you know? The two of us making each other braver, getting to a safe place. That'll never happen. I'm just alone and annoying and getting in the way. So I think for me it's really simple: I don't want to keep living. I want to change from living to not living, and I feel so good about this, Mom, I seriously do. But don't worry, I'll go slowly, and –

(**BASIL** *is there.* **JANE JR.** *hangs up.*)

Basil! Are you okay?

BASIL. Are you?

JANE JR. Yes yeah. Do you know where my mom is?

BASIL. I was hoping she was here.

JANE JR. What do we do?

BASIL. Maybe she is at the Celtic Knot or somewhere warm. I'll check everywhere.

JANE JR. *(Making his soft c a hard c.)* Celtic. Okay, I'll stay here in case she comes here.

BASIL. Okay great. Sounds great. I have to find her before the lady in the purple hat finds me. Bye.

JANE JR. Wait who's the lady in the purple hat?

BASIL. Who knows. The bridge between up here and down there. I'll make sure your mom gets home safe. Bye.

JANE JR. You're a hero!

BASIL. No I'm not. You asked me who am I. Who I am is: one day outta nowhere, I left my wife and children in Greece, that's who I am. Bye.

JANE JR. Wait Basil. Why'd you do that?

BASIL. Why?

JANE JR. Yeah.

BASIL. Because. Why? Because I... no. Fuck. Okay. Fuck. Because I... oh God.

(He inhales. He can't say it.)

JANE JR. You can say it.

BASIL. No I can't. Why? Okay. I left because.

(He looks at her.)

Because they wouldn't fucking leave me alone.

(He looks away from her.)

I don't want to be part of this anymore.

JANE JR. Wait, Basil. Thank you for telling me. When you walked in here, it got like twenty degrees warmer. Did you feel that?

BASIL. Oh, wow.

   (He leaves.)

JANE JR. It really did, I'm not kidding. Oh, zang, it's so hot. Oh whoa.

   (Now:)

   *(**MAIWORM** is sitting at the stretch of road where Peter's wife had her accident. We know it's the spot because there's so much salt there.)*

   *(The wind and the cold are unbearable. **BASIL** pushes against the vortex and finds **MAIWORM**.)*

BASIL. Maiworm, you'll freeze to death!

MAIWORM. Basil?

BASIL. Maiworm, I came to give you my heat. And I don't want you to blame yourself for what is about to happen.

   *(Suddenly, the **LADY IN THE PURPLE HAT** is behind **BASIL**.)*

   *(She whips **BASIL** around and speaks into his face. Then she whips him back around. Then she's gone.)*

MAIWORM. Ma'am? Ma'am?

   *(**BASIL**'s reeling. Dying.)*

Who was that? What did she say to you? Basil are you okay?

   *(**BASIL** hugs **MAIWORM**. He holds her as he falls.)*

BASIL. Am I her? Am I you? Are we fusing?

MAIWORM. Fusing?

BASIL. You're freezing up. Take my heat.

MAIWORM. Well I can't take your heat – you need it! Ah, oh God!

BASIL. I need to give it to you!

MAIWORM. Wow, it's so hot. It's burning up! Oh my God!

BASIL. Too hot?

MAIWORM. Not too hot!

BASIL. Uhhhhhhhhhhh

MAIWORM. Ahhhhhhhhhh

> (**BASIL** *takes* **MAIWORM** *down to the ground with him.*)

BASIL. *(Whispered.)* I'm sorry, I'm sorry

MAIWORM. Basil?

BASIL. I'm sorry, I'm sorry

MAIWORM. For what

BASIL. I'm sorry

MAIWORM. For what? Basil. Don't. Next year you move in with us.

BASIL. And then the next year I move out.

MAIWORM. But we're happy.

BASIL. Sometimes. You were the closest I ever felt to not running away.

MAIWORM. So stay.

BASIL. No.

MAIWORM. I don't understand. When is this happening?

BASIL. Silently one night outta nowhere.

MAIWORM. But why? Basil – no. Not you, Basil. I didn't know.

BASIL. You did know.

> *(He curls up. The road opens up.)*

And you must tell Peter not to follow me down.

MAIWORM. Oh no – Basil – HELP – oh Basil, you're –

You're just a little boy

You're just a little boy

> *(The wind dies down. **BASIL**'s gone. His body goes under the road.)*

> *(Silence. **MAIWORM** can't understand what's happening.)*

> *(**BASIL** comes up **JANE JACOBS**, who immediately starts muttering to herself and walking away from **MAIWORM**.)*

BASIL/JANE JACOBS. No, no, no! Horrible. Horrible, every second of it. Tearing up the road here. What is this, salt? Pah, pah.

> *(She spits out salt from her mouth. She keeps walking. **MAIWORM** walks after her.)*

Hole in this road. I hate people who tear up roads. Pah, pah.

MAIWORM. Excuse me ma'am, are you –?

BASIL/JANE JACOBS. Leave me alone.

MAIWORM. YOU'RE – Jane Jacobs?

BASIL/JANE JACOBS. Pah. Pah. Uck.

MAIWORM. Can I ask you – ma'am, I'm a tremendous fan. Can I ask you?

BASIL/JANE JACOBS. What is it?

MAIWORM. I'm trying – We're dying – skidding off –

BASIL/JANE JACOBS. What is the *question*?

MAIWORM. Should I do it? There's this new road de-icing technology. It would go under the roads – it would put people out of jobs, but it would go under the roads –

BASIL/JANE JACOBS. I don't know a damn thing about it. People die. People skid off. The ice melts. The ice conquers. Horrible fucking thing. No one allowed to see each other anymore. No one allowed to regenerate anymore. Why am I seeing this horrible thing? Why am I looking at you? Get away from me.

MAIWORM. Mrs. Jacobs –

BASIL/JANE JACOBS. Don't do anything. Dissolve. Walk around. And wait for it all to end.

MAIWORM. But Evanston needs me.

BASIL/JANE JACOBS. Bland town – already ruined – pah uck this salt –

MAIWORM. Evanston's not so bland. I just want to understand –

BASIL/JANE JACOBS. Stop it! Stop trying to understand! A city is organized *mystery*. If you can *understand* a city then it's already dead. I guess you want everyone dead! This place should be leveled!

MAIWORM. No, no! I don't! Don't say that about Evanston! This isn't like you, Mrs. Jacobs! You're an optimist!

BASIL/JANE JACOBS. No I'm not! You must not have read my later books!

MAIWORM. Oh God – I just want to fix the road!

BASIL/JANE JACOBS. Fine! Do what you want! Layering new sham on top of old sham, mistakes of the living on top of the mistakes of the dead. Fix the road, you pitiful administrator!

MAIWORM. No! Administration is *service*! Every day! That's what I *do*! I just keep chipping away at it – bit by bit – and if I get *specific* – things can be *solved*. Instead of all this – what is *this* – this waiting – just frigging *waiting*? Lie around and wait for the Big Horrible Unknown and then wake up, and there's a wall of water? Wake up, and we can't breathe, we're burning up? Wake up, and my husband's collapsed on the driveway, Bill Agrigento's hanging in the bathroom, my daughter's trapped inside herself, Peter's wife is dead on a road we *promised* her would be safe, and now Basil's, Basil's, where is he, what's happening... no! I can't! I'm not just going to wait. I want to wake up and fix some tiny things. A few tiny things. Get up and get to fixing some *specific tininess*, and then some specific tininess after that, and then our little nervousness will become a little happiness. It must, it must do that, while we're here, right? I think I have to believe that. And now that I've felt it, felt what Jane Jr. feels, the thing underneath everything, how big it is – I think I believe in tininess even more now. Get up and get to fixing. Like you did. Doesn't that seem valid?

BASIL/JANE JACOBS. My dear Jane, no. It's too late. I assure you. All of us in the invisible world already know it. Invisible cities sustained by the certainty of your extinction. All you can do is discover people. All there ever was was people. Discover your neighbors. Discover your children. When the sirens blare, you need to know each other, know where to gather, know each other's voices...

MAIWORM. Where are you going?

BASIL/JANE JACOBS. Horrible.

MAIWORM. Where's Basil?

BASIL/JANE JACOBS. That little boy? He died laughing under the road.

>(**MAIWORM** *is alone. In front of her, the road blazes with heat. She weeps. An approaching car honks –*)

>(*Now:*)

>(**JANE JR.** *is screaming.* **PETER** *hobbles into the room.*)

PETER. What happened?

JANE JR. I read a whole fucking book!!! It took me two fucking years!!!

PETER. That's wonderful. What was the book about?

JANE JR. The death and life of great American cities. And walking around and being STRANGE. I LOVED IT.

PETER. Can you be quieter? My daughter's sleeping in the other room.

JANE JR. Okay, sorry. She's really cute.

PETER. Okay. I have a confession. I ordered a pizza.

JANE JR. From where?

PETER. Domino's. They just put it in the oven. See?

>(*He shows her his phone.*)

JANE JR. Oh cool, the pizza tracker. Do you want to hear me sing?

PETER. Okay, yeah, sing. What are you gonna sing?

JANE JR. "Angel from Montgomery." Bonnie Raitt version.

PETER. Okay, great.

>(*Pause.*)

Are you gonna sing it.

JANE JR. Yeah. Can you turn around?

PETER. Sure.

(He turns around.)

JANE JR. Okay. How'm I gonna do this?

I AM AN OLD WOMAN,
NAMED AFTER –

I can't.

PETER. What?

JANE JR. I just can't do it.

PETER. Just do it. Sing.

JANE JR. I just can't.

PETER. Why not?

JANE JR. I don't know.

PETER. Just do it.

JANE JR. I can't do it. How?

PETER. Just the fucking doing.

JANE JR. No. I AM AN OLD WOMAN,
NAMED AFTER MY MOTHER
MY OLD MAN IS ANOTHER –

I can't.

PETER. WHAT?

JANE JR. I can't.

PETER. Yes you can.

JANE JR. No I can't haha

PETER. Yes you can haha

JANE JR. No

PETER. Yes

JANE JR. Fuck you

PETER. No fuck you

JANE JR. No fuck you

PETER. No fuck YOU

JANE JR. No fuck you haha

PETER. NO FUCK YOU!

Fuck you.

Fuck you. Fucking sing.

(He gets a call.)

One sec.

(He answers. He receives the following gravely.)

Hello? Oh. Really. Oh my God. Okay. Fuck. Is there anything I can do? Fuck, okay.

(He hangs up.)

That was Domino's. They can't deliver the pizza.

JANE JR. Why not?

PETER. It's too fucking vortexy.

JANE JR. *(Singing beautifully.)*

> I AM AN OLD WOMAN
> NAMED AFTER MY MOTHER
> MY OLD MAN IS ANOTHER
> CHILD WHO'S GROWN OLD
> IF DREAMS WERE LIGHTNING
> AND THUNDER WERE DESIRE
> THIS OLD HOUSE WOULD'VE BURNED DOWN
> A LONG TIME AGO

JANE JR.
>MAKE ME AN ANGEL
>THAT FLIES FROM MONTGOMERY
>MAKE ME A POSTER
>OF AN OLD RODEO
>JUST GIVE ME ONE THING
>THAT I CAN HOLD ON TO
>TO BELIEVE IN THIS LIVIN'
>IS JUST A HARD WAY TO GO
>THERE'S FLIES IN THE KITCHEN
>I CAN HEAR 'EM THERE BUZZIN'
>AND I AIN'T DONE NOTHING
>SINCE I WOKE UP TODAY
>HOW THE HELL CAN A PERSON
>GO TO WORK IN THE MORNING
>THEN COME HOME IN THE EVENING
>AND HAVE NOTHING TO SAY?

>(**PETER** *claps.*)

Thanks.

PETER. How old are you?

JANE JR. Thirty-one.

PETER. What the fuck?

JANE JR. What?

PETER. Why'm I babysitting you?

JANE JR. I don't fucking know!

PETER. Why'd your mom beg me to come here?

JANE JR. Because do you ever feel like your mom hates being around you?

PETER. Yeah. So?

JANE JR. Well and because I left her a weird voicemail.

PETER. About what?

JANE JR. ABOUT SUICIDE, PETER.

PETER. Are you suicidal?

JANE JR. Maybe.

PETER. I am.

JANE JR. Really?

PETER. Yeah.

JANE JR. Why?

PETER. Why are you?

JANE JR. Because I... I don't know because I don't

I can't

I don't

(Her fingers are flapping against her head.)

I want to...

(With her arms: "give & give & give.")

But instead I just...

(With her arms: "take & take & take.")

PETER. Listen I think, though, that, uh...you aren't actually gonna kill yourself silently one night outta nowhere. Maybe you just like looking at the shadow body of it? You want to touch it but not wanna marry it?

JANE JR. Says who.

PETER. Says me. I read this new micro-fiction story by Basil, I can send you the link. And in it, there's this character based on me. And he talks about suicide, but really what he's talking about is love for the invisible world. Or some shit. I need to read it again.

JANE JR. Oh, weird. That's – I want to read that.

PETER. I'll send you the link.

JANE JR. Thanks. Um, do you think there's something underneath everything that wants us to die?

PETER. 100%. I know it to be true.

JANE JR. Okay cool. Okay thanks. What I meant to say earlier is that I'm sorry about your wife. Not your life.

PETER. That's okay.

JANE JR. My dad died when I was sixteen.

PETER. Yeah. I remember when that happened. Fucking brutal.

JANE JR. Yeah.

PETER. Yeah. It all comes back brutal. Even the good stuff, you know? My wife she uh. She uh

JANE JR. Yeah

PETER. She, yeah, she would get so goofy it was like she became a different person. Like a goofy noodle. Just noodling around the house like a goofy noodle. Sometimes it would confuse me because she'd do it when things were weird, when the mood was bad, like we'd just had a fight or something. And I would get mad sometimes, thinking she was trying to send a message, like saying she hated how sad I was. Which maybe she did. But now I'm thinking about her eyes when she did it, she really just *became* a goofy noodle. Like me and my sad bullshit – coming outta nowhere. She couldn't help it. Just the goofiest fucking noodle. And why didn't I laugh more at it?

　　　(Pause.)

JANE JR. It's okay if you don't want to, but I really liked that, and I'm wondering if you'll tell me another story?

(He looks at her, and then reaches into his pocket and takes out a small booklet – five pieces of paper stapled together.)

What's that?

PETER. It's my favorite story ever.

JANE JR. Yes.

Read it.

PETER. "My daddy is a funny kid. His name is Peter Dad Oreos. Clak. He yells at a phone. Hivve? He works fo the snow. Once upon a time, was a dad. He hated about snow. Here is the truk, taller then a sky. The clouds are snow. The stars are salt. He climes forever. He scremms for us. The day was cold. But he got up and went outside. And I warm up. The end."

*(**MAIWORM** enters. She takes off her boots and hits the snow off them. She looks at her daughter.)*

MAIWORM. Are you okay?

The End

www.ingramcontent.com/pod-product-compliance
Lightning Source LLC
Chambersburg PA
CBHW072017290426
44109CB00018B/2272